Left or Right

Where's Eddie?

Daniel Nunn

Illustrations by Steve Walker

Hide and Seek

Raintree

Chicago, Illinois

www.capstonepub.com
Visit our website to find out
more information about
Heinemann-Raintree books.

To order:

☎ Phone 800-747-4992

🖳 Visit www.capstonepub.com
to browse our catalog and order online.

© 2013 Raintree is an imprint of Capstone Global Library, LLC
Chicago, Illinois

Edited by Dan Nunn, Rebecca Rissman, and Sian Smith
Designed by Joanna Hinton-Malivoire
Picture research by Mica Brancic
Originated by Capstone Global Library, Ltd. Production
by Victoria Fitzgerald

Library of Congress Cataloging-in-Publication Data
Nunn, Daniel.
Left or right : where's Eddie? / Daniel Nunn.
p. cm.—(Hide and seek)
Includes bibliographical references and index.
ISBN 978-1-4109-4712-3 (hbk.)
ISBN 978-1-4109-4718-5 (pbk.)

1. Vocabulary—Juvenile literature. I. Title.
PE1449.N776 2012
428.1—dc23   2012000354

Acknowledgments
We would like to thank the following for permission to reproduce
photographs: Shutterstock pp.5 (© Supertrooper), 6 (© Anna
Kucherova), 7 (© Katsai Tetiana), 8, 9 (© Audrey Ryou), 10 (©
Ihnatovich Maryia), 11, 12 (© Alekcey), 13, 14 (© Renata Osinska),
15, 16 (© Losevsky Pavel), 17, 18 (© PerseoMedusa), 19, 20 (©
Verdateo), 21 (© Iakov Kalinin), 22 (© Heiko Kiera), 23 (© Hamik).

Front cover photograph of pencils reproduced with permission of
Shutterstock (© Elnur).

Every effort has been made to contact copyright holders of any
material reproduced in this book. Any omissions will be rectified in
subsequent printings if notice is given to the publisher.

Printed in the United States   4964

Contents

Be careful when you hide!
Eddie can hide in places where people can't. Hiding inside things can be very dangerous. Always ask an adult if it is safe first.

Meet Eddie the Elephant

This is Eddie the Elephant.

Left and Right

Sometimes Eddie hides on the **left**.

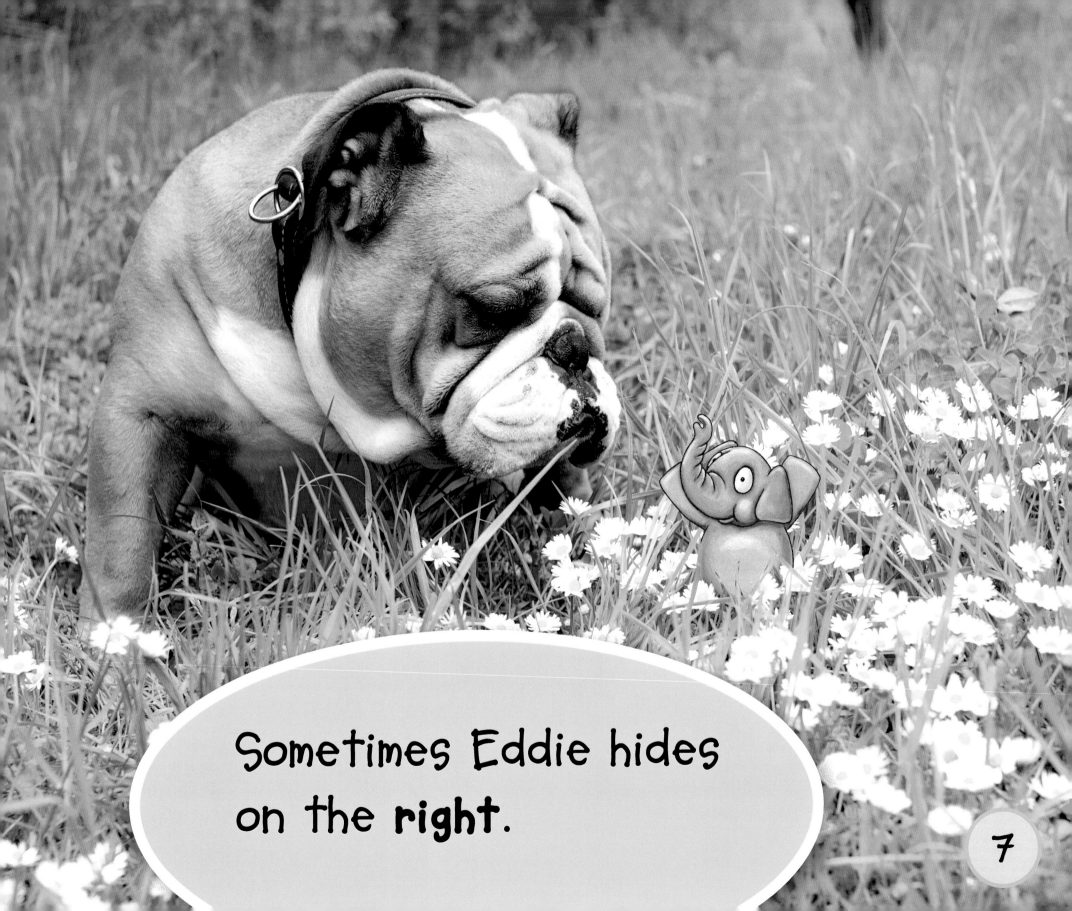

Sometimes Eddie hides on the **right**.

You can remember **left** from **right** using this trick. Hold out your hands like this.

The first finger and thumb on your left hand make an "L" for "Left." The fingers on your right hand don't make any letters!

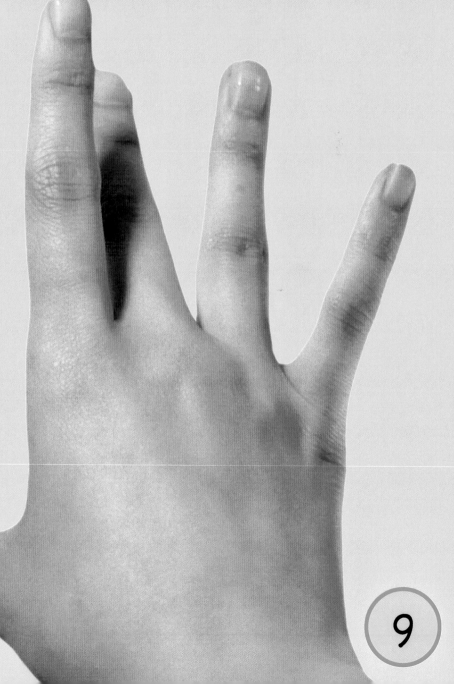

Find Eddie!

1 2 3 4 5 6 7 8 9 10

Can you find Eddie?
Count to 10, then off you go!

Where is Eddie? Do you see him to the **left** or to the **right** of the flowers?

11

Where is Eddie? Do you see him to the **left** or to the **right** of the boots?

Eddie is to the **right** of the boots.

14

Where is Eddie? Do you see him to the **left** or to the **right** of the truck?

15

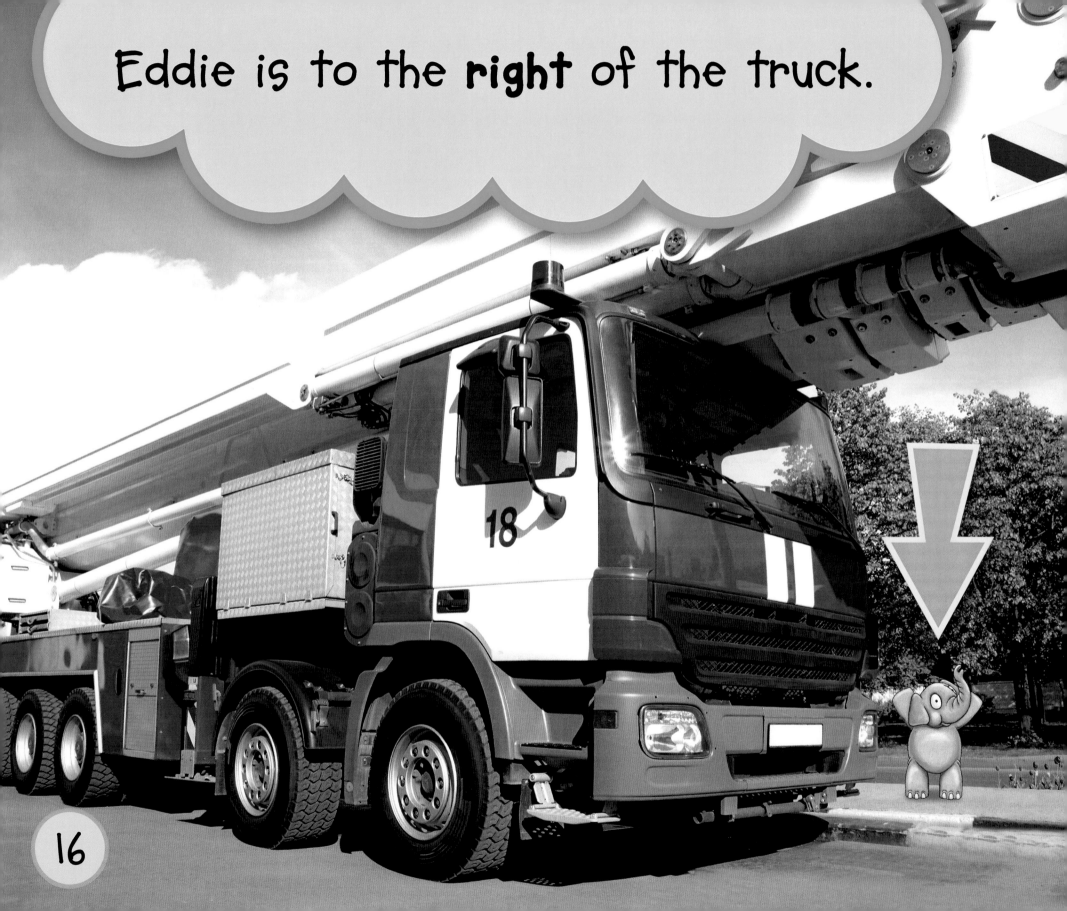

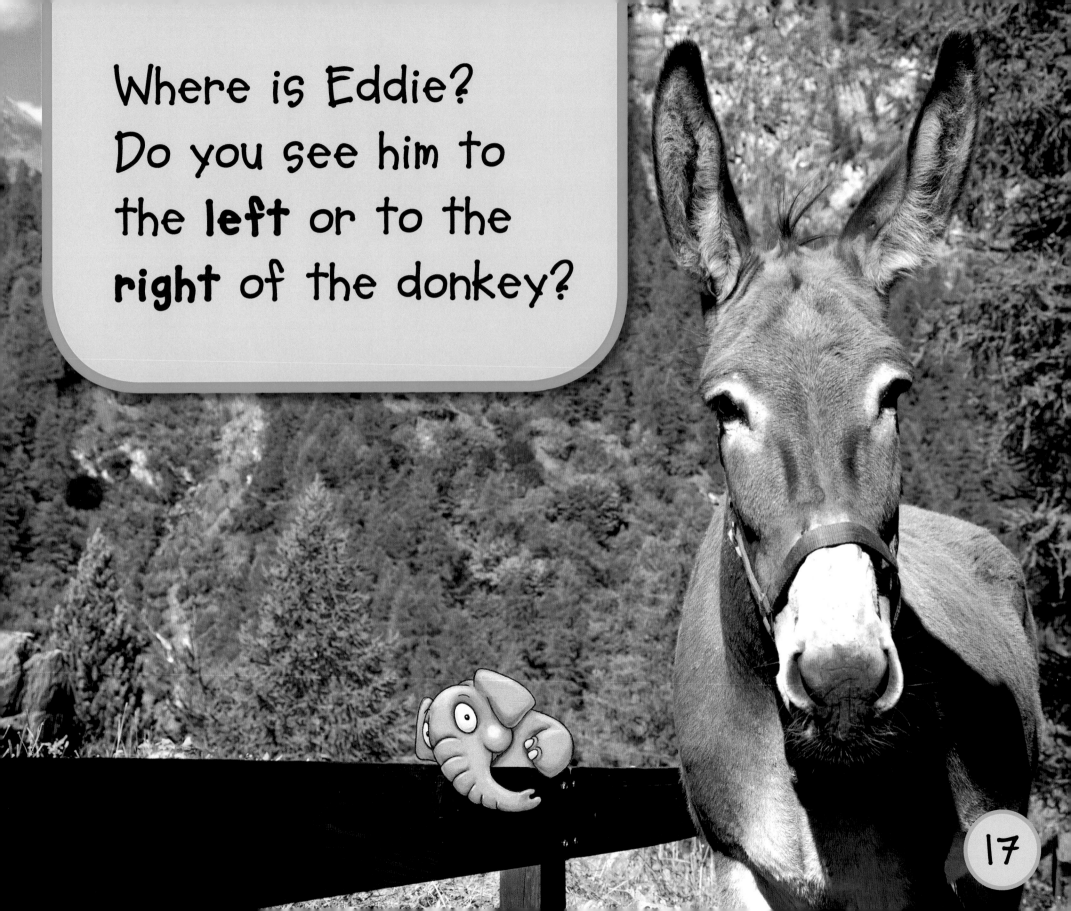

Where is Eddie? Do you see him to the **left** or to the **right** of the donkey?

17

Eddie is to the **left** of the donkey.

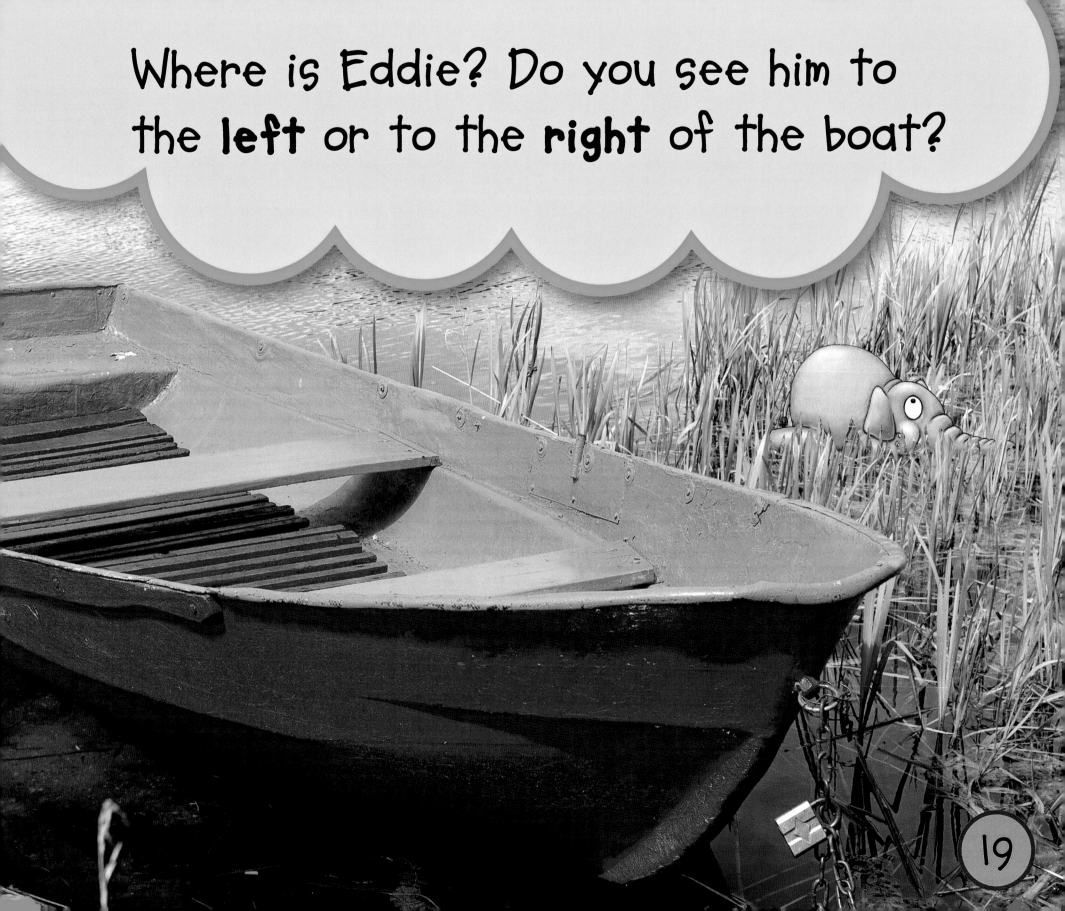

Where is Eddie? Do you see him to the **left** or to the **right** of the boat?

19

True or False?

1. We see Eddie to the **left** of the palm tree. True or false?

You can find the answers on page 24.

21

Answers and More!

True or false?

1. True! Eddie is to the **left** of the palm tree.
2. True! Eddie is to the **right** of the frog.
3. False! Eddie is to the **right** of the airplane.

Where can Eddie hide next?

Look around the room you are in.

What could Eddie hide to the **left** of?

What could Eddie hide to the **right** of?